DATE DUE	
	MAY 1 8 2012	JUL 0 5 2013	
	DISCARDED BY THE		
	URBANA FREE LIBRARY		

The Urbana Free Library

To renew: call 217-367-4057
or go to *"urbanafreelibrary.org"*
and select "Renew/Request Items"

MY
READING
LIBRARY

HUNGRY BUGS

by Ruth Owen

Editorial consultant: Mitch Cronick

NEW
FOREST
PRESS

CONTENTS

Words in **bold** are explained in the glossary.

Let's eat!

Hungry bugs like to eat.

Butterfly

4

Slurp!

Beetle

Munch!

Chomp!

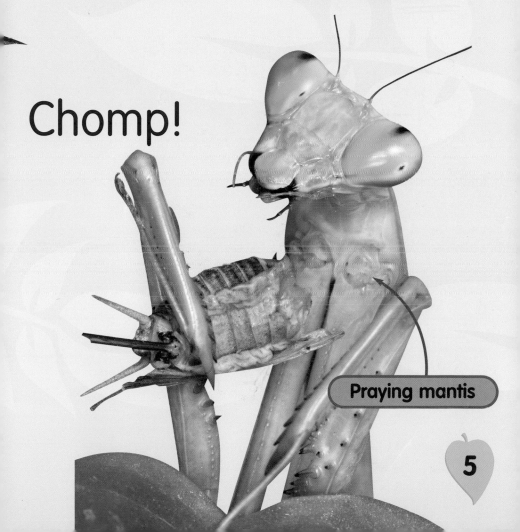

Praying mantis

Aphids

Aphids suck **sap** from plants.

6

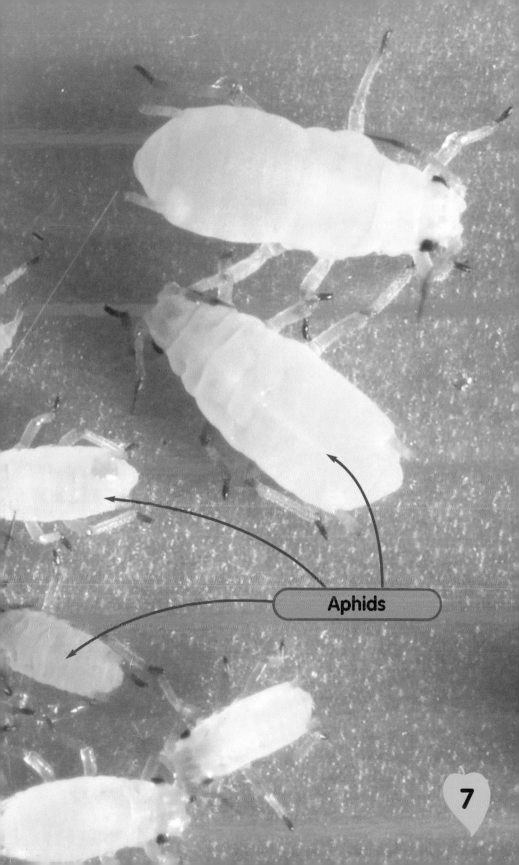

Aphids

Ladybugs

Ladybugs eat aphids.

Aphid

Ladybug

A ladybird eats 50 aphids in a day!

Leaf-cutter ants

These ants cut up leaves with their **jaws**.

Leaf

Leaf-cutter ant

They make ant food with the leaves.

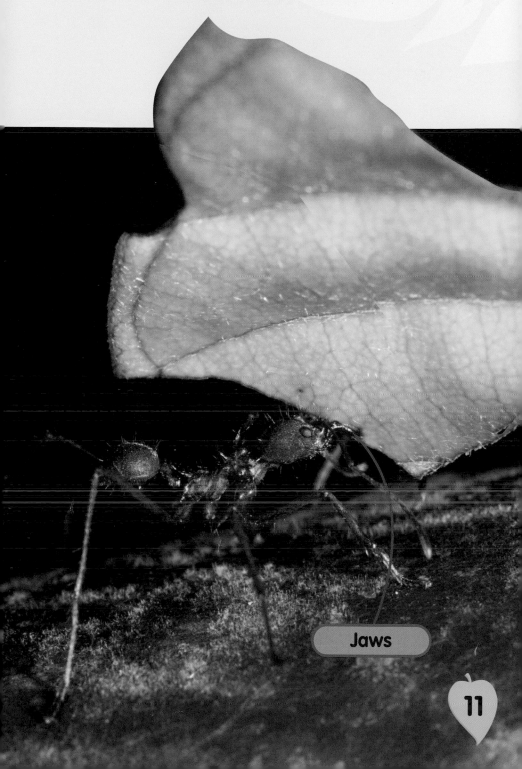

Jaws

Honeybees

Honeybees suck **nectar** from flowers.

Honeybee

Yummy honey!

Honeybees make **honey** with nectar.

Honeybee

Bee **larvae** eat the honey.

Larvae

We can eat the honey too!

Honey

Munch, crunch, lunch!

Caterpillars eat plants.

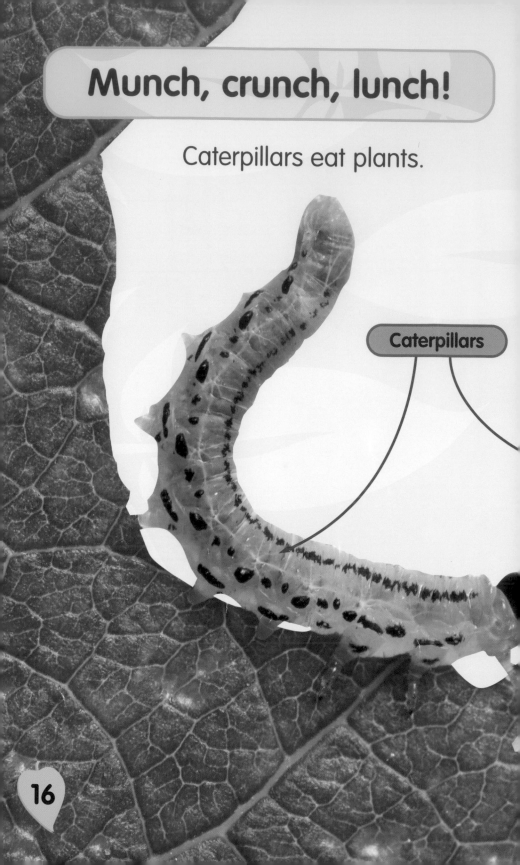

Caterpillars

Butterflies

Caterpillars turn into butterflies!

4

3

2

1

18

Butterfly

Butterflies suck nectar from flowers.

Dung beetle

This **dung** beetle eats elephant poo!

Poo

Elephant

Dung beetle

21

Glossary

dung
A word for animal poo.

honey
A thick, sweet foo
made by bees.

jaws
Parts of an ant's head
that it uses to bite.

larvae

The young (babies) of some bugs.

nectar

Sweet, runny stuff that comes from flowers.

sap

Runny stuff made by plants.

23

Index

Publisher: Melissa Fairley
Studio Manager: Sara Greasley
Editor: Emma Dods
Designer: Trudi Webb
Production Controller: Ed Green
Production Manager: Suzy Kelly

North American edition copyright © TickTock Entertainment Ltd. 2010
First published in North America in 2010 by New Forest Press,
PO Box 784, Mankato, MN 56002
www.newforestpress.com

ISBN 978-1-84898-379-3
Library of Congress Control Number: 2010925600
Tracking number: nfp0007
Printed in the USA
1 3 5 7 9 10 8 6 4 2